salmonpoetry
Publishing Irish & International
Poetry Since 1981

the **arts council** an chomhairle ealaíon

funding **literature**

artscouncil.ie

dairena ní chinnéide
deleted

Published in 2019 by
Salmon Poetry
Cliffs of Moher, County Clare, Ireland
Website: www.salmonpoetry.com
Email: info@salmonpoetry.com

ISBN 978-1-912561-78-0

Cover Artwork: *"Deleted" by Jeaic Ó Cinnéide Pender – Instagram: ciaej_art*
Cover Design & Typesetting: *Siobhán Hutson*

Printed in Ireland by Sprint Print

Salmon Poetry gratefully acknowledges the support of
The Arts Council / An Chomhairle Ealaíon

To those who connected along the way and made the journey of this book so precious. Go raibh maith agaibh ar fad.

Níl in aon ní ach seal.

Contents

Unplugged on the Great Blasket

Heat rises in waves
on the empty sand
of An Tráigh Bhán
particles of social history
float like phantoms
constantly shifting
leaving patterns of something precious
for us to interpret.

Time becomes abstract
the tide bursts
in rhythmic roars
on this craggy shore.

The displaced anxiety
of being off the grid
the luxury of a bed
wraps around us
like a selkie's cloak.

Sunset sweeps the horizon
the high tide line
an electric pathway
around the mainland peninsula
chalk white
against sea blue.

We are but flotsam
in the ancient folklore
of this island's people
we tread with care
we give thanks for it.

The Seal's Song

The noise of seals
crying
as they came ashore
for the night
they sense
the retreat of humanity
singing as they roll
from the sea
to An Tráigh Bhán
a ribbon of bright pink on the horizon
conceals itself
then darkens a little
they leave their trace on sand
we light the spark within us.

Nightlights in Peig's House

I write by candlelight
seals keen on a night blue beach
seagulls fly low
this island of lost souls
terrifying in it's beauty
a breath golden sound
soothes the strain
lulls you into contemplation
the isolation
loses and finds its moorings
in this half life
a submerged presence
on a lost island.

Making Hay

Sun splits
like over ripe fruit
bursting in a summer bowl
strains of calm classical tones
run through the growth
bees hover over red clover
the lady's smock has died
alters full of hope
stand like crisp reminders
of the joy of golden buttercups
blossoming in the wild
never mowed or plucked
simply to behold
warmth rises in tiny freckles
on the pallor of a long winter
seashells of ancient seas
bask on the beach
not collected or trodden
remnants of beauty
waiting for a full tide
silverweed hugs the patio stone
in the lush wild garden.

The Chieftain's Call

And so they go
the chieftains passed
they may have made challenging parents
lost in their minds, their art
they loved like they thought they ought to.

I call them chieftains too
the mothers who created art
between cooking and rearing
making and crafting
weaving legacies.

Children's minds
have off kilter memories
where structure means chaos
creation casts loss
like living on another frequency.

My chieftains have passed on
but more live with me alive
books like sentries
shine brighter than a headstone
wondering how we live our lives

in frequent isolation
we withdraw
to continue to create
to craft something new
to learn with respect from the chieftains.

Rí Rá

for Liam Carson

There was a hubbub in the corner
like impulsive currents of electricity
a drunken woman roaring at a drunker man
projected poison verbally flung
mischief thunders through the late night crowd
as Saturday night in a *síbín* surrenders to strife.

Rumblings of discord shatter banter
an uproar of pushing and shoving
tangles all the energy in the air
some stand back to observe
others throw a belt with knuckled fist
for some past wrongdoing or slur on the family
the invited new guest at the row
pummels back smack in the stomach
energised now to let off some steam

men and women clatter and bite
the throng amoeba like sways left
a stool goes flying
the spectators grinning with impish laughter
fodder for the Sunday morning
post Mass melee gossip out the back of the church.

This *rí rá* and *ruaille buaille*
is a cultural expression
it will become the stuff of legend
the fusion of booze and giddiness
there'll be no harm done
it's just letting off steam.

The offended woman
surrounded by a gaggle of girls
tearfully and verbally vomits
her side of the sorry story
they sympathise loudly
no man would cross this boundary
she's almost forgotten what all the fuss was about
delighted with the chance to bate yer man
the bloody husband, the bane of her life.

The men have a good old laugh
huddled by the only Guinness tap
straddled on an old barrel in the corner
as it settles, so do they
great slagging and handy bars ensues
as the offended man knocks back half a pint
thirsty after the scrap
the lads are careful not to insult the wife
'tis family business after all

a hidden house on the *rí rá*
an old fashioned gathering
where music rips off the rafters
nimble dancers
grown from the tumult, spark the stone floor

'Tis mighty *craic* all the same
all tension dispelled
everyone is happy
to tell the tale of the uproar
as a source of mirth on some long night
where the wrangling seems like a phantom
rising godlike with the dawn
as the party strolls home.

Sí [sh-e]

: of her; fairy; bewitching; enchanting :

She is she
of fairies
       female

sí is *sí*
of otherworld
       fancies

she is she
of magic
       flesh

sí is sí
of spells
       fortuitous

she is she
of turbulence
       frothy

sí is sí
of herself
       frolicksome

she is she
of dreams
       frenzied

sí is *sí*
of all she wishes to be:
       free.

Corrib I

All the deaths that I have died
by wallowing waters
angry rivers blowing silt brown
magic lakes with islands of remorse
high sad cliffs, dizzy from vertigo
I died a little bit by them all
wondering if there would be an end
clinging like a child to a sad poem
exploring the possibilities of the soul
while white foam and wind
exploded in my troubled heart.

Corrib II

There amidst a ganglion of Gaelic writers
I sat like a suckling calf
by the shiny teats of my books
an imposter of an ancient order
relatively fresh from the poetic womb
quietly uttering something distinctive
slightly in awe of the chieftain's
casually chatting for TG4
celebrating seventy years of Kennys
a dwarf in a tall institution
shyly becoming a cow.

Departure

Like shedding skin
fragments are packed up
shards of sanctuary disappear
the cottage dishes are washed
bags negotiate themselves
in a form of farewell.

I sit in this artists retreat
observing beauty peeking out of a Lidl's bag
almost completed paintings
of a desire
as transitory as the brushstroke
the intentional randomness
of a splattered and empty easel.

Colours echo more than sound
or the potential of memory
from the artistry within us
swallowed gulps of gaiety
a whole moon on a shoulder
the palette of parting
still wet in cracks of stone.

Dúchas

It's in your bones, your DNA
like a scrap at a county final
an indelible cognisance
of your heritage.

Your name carries
serious consequences
discussions on lineage
or what a great man your father was.

It's knowing the name
of every field in your village
or the unique way each of your neighbours
brings the cows home.

It's the Irish language
pouring out of our hearts
the subtle nuances between parishes
that make our sacred code.

It's pure tribalism
bent over a pint in a parish pub
it's slurs on handy bars
bursting over a mighty song.

To belong is to have pride
to love every cliff and peak
to respect the sense of ritual
to live in a community.

It lets wild men be wild
and worthy women sing on high stools
while beady eyes peer
in moral judgement.

To walk those hills in a wind
to blow the isolation from your brain
to fill your heart with beauty
is to give thanks for the privilege.

It's the unspoken tongue
that guides your sense of identity
it's every fibre that makes you, you
it lets you belong, when you are blue.

The Gaelic Lover

The perfect lover
would be fluent
in Irish
teachin' a learner
has three wheels
none of them stable
it chaffs like
beard rash
sandpaper on a petal.

The perfect lover
would conjugate
his tenses
in primal utterings
his adjectives and nouns
would agree perfectly
the copula would always be
in the present tense
evading the conditional mood
and his cardinal directions
would be crystal clear.

The perfect lover
sings the perfect tune
a lullaby of love
that tells you
his banter
is natively believable
you know the tune
and move accordingly
on a recognisable page
syncopated rhythms
you snatch syllables from
to suit yourself.

The perfect lover
leaves like Irish
in the morning
when the rest of life
invades your condition
post coital language paralysis
eclipsed nouns
straying around in your head
like vagrants
dispossessed of their identity.

He doesn't exist
like the perfect scholar
of the official standard rules
a deserter
from an army of irregular verbs
titillating your senses
into a false sense of security
directing relative clauses
with no subject
leaving you shadowed
in the negative form
unfulfilled
eternally translating
from Irish to English
and from English to Irish
in search
of the perfect buzz
in any language.

Fairy

At times she lives between the leaves of weeds
she doesn't discriminate
a rose or a *buachallán buí*
there is no nitrate in her magic dust
to grow is to be beautiful.

Then with fragrant wine
she turns it into nectar
berry by berry
making liquid heaven
to write for her is pleasure.

To seek her out
is bad manners
she must always come to you
a flash of dreams on a dull day
to delight you with her fairy power.

She is a childish secret
lurking in the foundations of adulthood
reserve magic
when life gets too much
to rise above it all and dance.

She is translucent time
shimmering on the edges of things
an overall sense sensation
dribbling letters in shiny ink
to soothe the absent in your soul.

West Kerry Morning

Daylight sharpens on stale dreams
I'm electrified suddenly by the light
an illuminated patchwork of fields
shining under a winter sun.

I awake in awe of those hills
neon cliffs beckon a new day
brewing coffee with hope
to soothe the sleepy music within.

I rise in wonder of starlings
the view like a womb
ancient towers stand to my attention
every glorious peak sings.

The high tide line has been breached
this came from the belly of the sea
a ritual incantation of words
to ignite my Sunday morning

and when the tide lies low
I'll walk the wet sand of my poem
absorb its salt for another day
until one day it will implode into frothy waves.

Unbelievably Myself

(A Rant)

How hard
the pretense of ordinary existence
the exhaustion of maturity
I cannot do life
when my head exists
in a parallel universe.
I do not wish to dance
to the strain of conformity.
My life is a long apology
for being who I am.
I did not choose to be a poet
some primal fissure
in my fragmented mind
split and erupted in me
fuelled on the cerebral adrenalin
that ignites the obscure clarity
of poetic thought.

I like jigsaws with missing pieces
I draw the damaged and the damned
for I am their equal in hurt
the specters of known and unknown souls
born without the second skin
designed to protect us from the cruelty of life
solving my puzzle
as words call me
weaving a lexical leash
to tame the wild creature I am.

Zipping up the leather boots of anarchy
I overthrew the bondage of origin
shaved off the shit of denial
shunning hate and lies
stupidity and gossip.
I write my own constitution
where all the bye laws are in verse
my articles of association swear allegiance
to the iridescent surges of art
a divine congress of creativity.

I preside over a Supreme Court
where love, passion and beauty
are not punishable crimes
a land where all expression is joy
in a gentle democracy of grace
embracing difference
as something of true value.

This is the path I chose
to learn with an open heart
to reveal that which is concealed
sheltering in solitude
from the showers of commentary
a pure soul
on a cosmic roadtrip
doing my best to function
in a world I never understood
reconciling myself with reality
with the alphabet of eternal hope
at my fingertips.

Hybrid

Grey smoke rises
from my neighbour's chimney
blasted by angry wind
the corpse of my day
cremated into sticky rain
sucking me dry
my thoughts
locked into the raging storm.

The wheelie bin
of my imagination
blown sideways
just abstract rubbish
whirling outside the window.
I struggle for focus
as beleaguered scraps
scatter at the gable.

I cannot fight
this storm
knowing only
the linguistic choice:
today
English is my beacon
it summons itself
but Irish is the wind
howling outside.

A force of nature
chattering in my ear
distracting my thoughts
reminding me who's boss.

To gust
in hidden eddies
lurking in the vortex
of language choice
exploring the untrodden
in my hybrid vehicle
getting lost in the storm
knowing my tongue
will always guide me home.

Irish & The State

It's like the longest game of football
in the history of the state
a bunch of men and women
slithering around in the muck
on a rainy Sunday afternoon
the other team wearing their suits
on the pitch
they were on overtime anyway
the game was being held
wasn't that proof enough
of their commitment?

Personnel would change
and new rules made
the spectators dying of boredom
while the referee argued
grammatical points
stalling the progress of the game
until years and years later
the team supporters
went blue with resentment
tired of time wasting
and preferential treatment
a tedious burden
slathered in hypocrisy.

Eventually the game petered out
so they set up a special committee
to draw up new rules
a benchmark strategy
how to save the game
in a big plan
to recognise the home grounds
in every community
where a game could be played.

Above and below the border
change was happening
a new game was set up in Europe
on home turf there was now a trendy pride
a Gaelic rap-fest at half time
urban followers now chanting
in the first language
the Aussie rules of Irish
breaking barriers
the feeling for the first time
that your team would score
a sense of pride and identity
in this ancient art form
while the suits scurry in the background
ticking the boxes
giving back to the people
something they already owned
the language the game was invented in.

The Contradiction of Fertility

Feminine and still fertile
suspended
looking at calendar dates
willing blood flow
only women welcome pain like
that raw cramp
which is the portent to
menstruation
another close shave
when you pray to God
you'll never have sex again
if only the blood would come

some of us are sentries
to our body clocks
delicate mechanisms
subject to lunar songs
dictating physical time zones
of fertility
issuing boarding cards
according to the flight path
of our eggs
trying to avoid collision
with conception.

five to midnight
with the maternal softness
of woman
I place a loving hand on my belly
and dance a dance of love
I chose to own my choice
to dictate the consequences
of what might be something after all
something I cannot give

then suddenly
in the abstract motion of Gods
I feel the fresh vindication of blood
relief like corking champagne
another cautionary catastrophe
the consequence
of what I thought was love
but turned out only to be another illusion

that fiction formed in women
who ignore the power of their own bodies
when lost in the fickle arms
of transient desire
craving only love
and not the creation of life.

The October Revolution

This lack of emotion is alarming
my fairies have been
repossessed by NAMA
the very state I vote for
is gunning for me
for being a depressed poet
who doesn't keep accounts.

My love is
like Foucault's Pendulum
swinging dangerously
in and out of my fragile heart
a swoop too far
for I capitulate
I can barely cope with myself.

My frontline are singing cantos
in tune with hails of phantom bullets
we are all bored with the war
my *Aurora* fired only poetry
at governmental lack of style
for the proletariat are prisoners
of state stupidity
our proud red guards sleep in social inertia.

I bore holes in my tired brain
looking for my inner Bolshevik
but it is dead
and I'm living in the wrong era
numb from trying
and getting shot down.

What a country
to be depressed in
strung out in apathy
in each others arms
but there's no one there
except light and day.
to rely on.

My Winter Palace
has been stormed
by demonic crows
looking for my slice pan.

I rise and smile
and cry in defiance
starting my own October Revolution
in my heart
where brutality and oppression
are only chocolate sprinkles
on an overthrown cake
laced with the resilience, of a woman at war.

Wellness

It is a subtle shift
tremulous notes like star music
filtering gently into that murky space
that obscures the path to happiness
a celestial symphony of pure joy
quivering through eddies of sadness
lifting the spirit towards clarity
from the lonely precipice
only an echo remains
of that ancient song you thought defined you
before you knelt before the Gods of wisdom
and sought the taste of the well of truth
no more the dance of destruction
for now you choose your own guides
to hold your hand out of respect
in a circle of true friendship
empowering you to love and be loved
in this sacred life spun with threads of pure gold.

Morning Raga

I salute the sun
from a stone seat
to see the sea
through a corridor of ruins
an awakening mind
breathing with the breeze
warm skin songs
body touching keys
to sound notes of instinct
on invisible ivory and black
scales become sentences
not rehearsed but born
innate articulations
like tiny unraveled mysteries
form absconds from structure
winged like something unseen
light becomes meaning
in the divine sanctuary
Gods descend
unknowns blossom in knowing
weeds attain perspective
purpose becomes being
like a fathomless soul
finding home.

deleted

My message was acknowledged
but he didn't recognize the number
I am deleted.

Hurts at times
when you get what you want.

The Warrior Mother as Muse

Your journey is a vessel
filled with the blood of birth

full of the amniotic fluid
red hot with protective foam

and you carry it
from conception to growth

your hands burned
by the heat of motherhood

the birth chord
cut by the world on your behalf

but you know
as the sisterhood of fairies know

it is your lifeline
your masculine and your feminine

as commander and friend
you sit on a tall ocean reef

in the middle of the sea
with no lifeline except your self belief

filling the vessel now
with the flotsam of storm on dark nights

keeping your own counsel;
your muse, your articulation

flowing in a stream of words
then with rising sun and school sandwiches

the warrior in you strengthens
in a wave of energy

nurturing your seed
filling the vessel with pure love.

The Warrior on the Run

i

The Warrior floated in the heavens
without a care in the world
a depth of brownish hue
on the fading green ferns
a soft yellow greyness
lapping the nettles
on the cliff top
the bleating of waves
electric blue
the lullaby of white foam
laughing in her ears.

ii

The sea rose
under the silver shadow of the sun
cold, biting and whistling
through the door
forming a sharpness
in the shimmying alphabet
of her mind.
She was at peace
in this clifftop cave
jazz and sanctuary
hanging like silk
from her body.

iii

The night-time sky
a cauldron of black
the ecstasy of aloneness
a twinge of guilt
as if neglecting
the burdens of life
but it was only
an odd seashell
prattling wind
lichen on rocks.

On the full moon night
the Warrior was alone
walking by the cliff
the storm abated
she felt like
seabirds.

The Quivering Warrior

Kind sleep eluded her
for a week
in liminal flight over her threshold
taking lunar form
so full of desire
streams of sweetness
ran through
the Warrior felt the trace of her
man
unsteady with love
she drank it in
she welcomed it
she let him loose with his longing
until she herself felt a thirst
until their limbs connected
until the quivering came
then she rested.

Purple Day

The day falls to purple
evening sky blushes
that wintry crisp
of pink and pale blue
you oscillate between shades
of hysterical emotion
black is death and hurt
purple is passion
cold unleashes in waves
the day is unpredictable
it is almost always thus
sunsets make you cry
you weep for the broken willow branch
life seems overwhelming
purple brings you alive
colouring your mood
to rise up and just be purple.

Pain as Myth

i Pre Hospital Visit

Couch curled like coal-dust, comfort my abstraction, a vague
irksome aura about my body, some unknown manifesting itself,
a sign that perhaps that the sins, the manifold badness of a
past life, have found form in my present self, a known mystery
only the hospital I sick to tomorrow may unravel, ache like a
muffled scream that hasn't found it's voice, appearing and
disappearing in a random pattern, like a tune playing itself
on a scratched disk, a deep flow, echoing in my psyche, like
an unfinished mythology

ii Hospital Outpatients

A black sea of shoes, huddle in Waiting Area 1
fractured static from the TV on the wall, an hour and
a half I've concealed myself in a book, trying to appear well
adjusted, but the woman with the red hands scratches herself
obsessively and it's hard to maintain equilibrium, I don't know what
I am doing here, I have a mystery inside me, babies shriek,
at the desk I wobble at a question that has bent me before:
next of kin: nobody.

iii Myth

Hours of penned sheep passivity later it seems I am an administrative
error, my mystery is "not in the consultant's area of expertise" and my
medical records, bizarrely, ten years out of date, typical,
past my sell by date in diagnostic data, I'm discharged, like an
animal no one would buy at auction, my mythology still incomplete.

A Day for Dylan

It was a day for Dylan
dark, wild and treacherous
staccato heartbeats
blown in swirls of confusion
like the angry wind outside
a love storm that wreaked havoc
on my equilibrium
sick of it
just sick of all this love
gluttonous and gloomy
fateful and still
like a Greek tragedy
that has no end.

Framed

I knew the day
I hung the painting
I'd hang us too.

Suspended on my wall
his imprint
on my privacy.

Who could contain
such chaos
waiting for a tidal change
to release or drown me.

Unlike the artist
the art is mine
it was a gift.

I did not foresee its weight
a thing of such beauty
and destruction
contained
unlike my feelings
under a pane of glass
staring at each other
until one of us is broken.

Detached

The emotional house
was semi detached
walls slowly crumbling
on foundations of hope
full of faults
fissures of hurt
seeped into the mortar
camel's blood
would not bind them
for they were haunted
unfulfilled past lives
the strain of love
too great a burden
for the day in day out fallout
of botched behavioral patterns
repetitive errors
it became too hard
to change the record
suddenly the emotional house
lost the cause and detached
preferring the company of crows
practiced at recovery
she flew away
leaving him the house
to deal with.

Off Day

Radiohead give me the karma police in my brain. Thunder-foam lashes the day's rocks on a headland that is upside down with refracted meaning. Storm inclines inward in howls. Rubbish shoots like fake bunnies on the track between not so social housing. A mean day. I am the sound the wind makes, angry and sad and lost and losing my temper in the lost and never found compartment of futile exercises. Hell is a cold council house where there is no happiness. Heaven is central heating. I don't have that. My solid fuel has converted itself to emotional mulch and paranoia pours out over the pot I simmer to declare indifference. Treachery lurks in the clouds I know to be a depressing omnipotent grey, through semi-opaque window blinds I leave eternally drawn. My mood is off.

Nights of disturbed non-sleep. Vignettes of dreams project in a short subconscious fringe festival no one is watching except me. I don't understand these films. Not really. I am both main actor and crowd, a voyeur of my own desperate darkness. They prescribe pills, but that anarchist in my chemical makeup defiantly refuses to step back and let them do their thing. My brain like an overdriven head gasket that blows and blast-guns any hope of steady throttle in all those hours of darkness. It isn't always thus, but right now, like for days and days it's just me being the cuckoo on the clock, making a center stage appearance on the hour on the half hour, waking me from respite. It's exhausting. Sixty minutes in my dark head is like a lifetime. I am utterly alive at every wakeup call that crazy cuckoo pecks me awake with. Nerves fray. I feel unhappy. Restless. Afraid.

When one is having an off day, the feeling is akin to being wasted. The fluffy, shifting shape in and out of disgusting reality. Who wants reality? I am too irksome for people today. I'd only be critical and picky and catty or too talkative and dramatic and overpowering. Never the bloody middle ground with me. So other people's melodies carry me along with the dark day outside. It doesn't feel much different to the night. Just the expectation of having to answer a phone and even in polite exchanges I manage to cause damage. I am projecting sharp, sore, nails at the world, coz inside I'm hurting.

My embedded she wolf has been bitten by the daily challenge of existence. I am howling soundlessly. Years have taught me no one wants to hear the cries of a wounded animal. It's best to put them out of their misery. I ponder the mercy of making the human variety writhe in translucent pain - to carry the proverbial cross whilst simultaneously nailing oneself to it, to prove the multitasking facility of being a once functioning and sometimes brilliant person. No, it's defiantly more humane to kick back, wrapped around a warm blanket, woolly socks, several layers of warm jumpers and hoodies, plugged into music that reflects a pixilated state of mind, very loud, but curiously quiet.

Soothed, I relish this hidden day. Drifting around my damaged state, feeling the safety of being alone. Fashioning a cage from my fragility. But the bars are made of sugary substances I can melt with my mind like a spell caster, whirly gigging in secret.

Convention just sounds like a really silly word. Having heating systems on my mind I think of convection and distribution, but am clear in the knowledge that none of that has the remotest connection to the way I really think. *Massive Attack* is my aural yoga now, my sun salutation, lifting my spirit in a really cool and kind of mysteriously surreal way. My pose is peculiar and it turns raindrops into crystals kissing my bedroom windowpane. The tragedy of the day becomes external. Wasted now I seem not to care as much about the anger of the storm. I see beauty in the words it blows around my purring brain. This part of my day becomes an act of defiance. A meditation on being. Then later, pampered with an abstract kind of hue, I will become domestic. I will light a fire. I will cook dinner. I will will the hours and dart through another night, tired but alive and ready to be surprised by an emotional change of direction. Wandering happily, like a nymph in a *Dr. Who* telephone box towards some kind of happy equilibrium.

Spring Equinox

Far over golden sands
the Sphinx turns it's face
towards the rising sun
this Vernal Equinox.

Brandon capped in snow
cold spins in the air
as a sunbeam penetrates
a narrow stone passage.

A fertile lovemaking
as the spirits of the Gods dance
in our off kilter minds
the coming of Spring.

We are rejoicing
an equal night
our bodies sway
hanging in the balance

Feoghanagh

A flock of brent geese fly
black feathered, white bellied moving
from the storm exposed estuary
in twilight over the beach
to the Artic circle

I am gripped by the sight
the cliffside transformed
by blowing gale and crumbling rock
it's high path dangerous
like the journey of the geese

a river that ever flowed one way
bending in renewed shape
the brent getting out of town
from eternally changeable weather
in this harsh, steadfast, place

they head for Greenland
to get a break
from constant storms
from the sun's doubt
ever falling rain

an immigrant family
fleeing from lack of love
like a silken black sky etching
arresting my mind
leaving a print of dark colours.

Flying the Coop

Flown coop,
a wall
between emptiness;

space expands
in this narrow
house;

I do not inhabit
just resting
conjuring my nest;

aloneness
blares
digitally enhanced;

oneness
breathes personality
comet risen;

I blossom
by dim light
in my bed;

loverless
ecstatically naked
like water;

purified silence
delves in
I live alone alive.

Numinosity

for Síle Denvir

I see sketches of islands
half revealed
like deities
in a haze
sun shines on sea
like errant particles
glittering
in their own glory
the presence
of numinous beings
reflect off the surface
brown rushes
turn gold
on cliffs.

Solstice Wind

Strange rafters
making a music
I have not heard before
in bed alone content
to leave the log wood embers
crackling in the night
this short sun
listening to a hidden moon
sing it's longest song
drinking a feast of warm port
dreaming of Saturanalia
robbed by a Christian child
to behold our day of feasting
I am enchanted by midwinter
nestled under the eaves
predicting happy dreams
joyous and peaceful
drifting on a different
abstraction of peace within
this solstice night
at home with holly berries.

Domus

Home is a place
where there is no fear
I have left fear
behind me
to delve into magic.

Home is a haven
where no one peers
through estate windows
at my inability
to feel at home.

Home is sanctuary
to lie and listen to wind
and not be afraid
of losing my mind
in an unhappy space.

Home is where
my mind flows with ease
when sorrow is left behind
like an unsung song
making new music.

Ritual

Wintry wind
reefs through leaves of grass
I look out my kitchen window
to see a stone circle.

Stretching my body on a central slab
the energy funnels
to the six large rocks of stone
that sit waiting.

They pause for knowing souls
to reap the power
of this secluded spot
calling to the gods.

Those beings, fresh and ancient
release within me a creativity
of substance and soul
in this sacred space I now call home.

Mozart's Requiem

Pure music wafts around the room
folds upon folds of sound
complexities of mood
the human condition in D minor
wrapping itself round you
softening like ripe flesh
rising in a crescendo
epic in its flight
listening is pure joy
you break down in a movement
falling slowly
you release yourself
through vocal clouds
deep baritones seduce you
scores of violins savage you
to the point of ecstasy
your thoughts dissipate
now there's only music
to move your soul
now you are naked with every note
bare but beautiful
blessed with this sound
you surrender to symphony
you cry out loud
sounds like psychic imprints
from a childhood of music and mystery
trip you out
like an angel
having an out of body experience.

The Hairy Goat

To wake and weave
the crooked legs of a goat
from your morning hair
missing the teeth
of the night before
slightly chipped
aching like the fusion
of booze and giddiness
crawling around your brain
like deserters from a cause
of good intentions
an irregular evening
off the couch
into the social network
chatting with randoms
electrically charged
human exchanges
in the smoking zone
then descending
into the depths
of a packed small pub
like uncorked champagne
ordering a round
at the crowded counter
ready to explode
with sheer delight
then it gets patchy
a chattering taxi driver
on a vague journey home
in the morning
light refracts in your eyes
a vampire in daylight
who sucked the blood
out of a good night out

staring cockeyed
at you in the mirror
hangover complete
then you brush the goat
from your hair
with the flourish
of a seasoned professional
and crawl back to bed.

Witch in the Mirror

I see a fiery red raven
between the mirror and I

I am absent
cast in a net of thoughts

she flies about the white room
under the rafters of my home

where sleep eludes me
like a cat underwater

slippery shadows
in my minds eye

she's risen up
sparks in her wings

flapping
at the end of the bed

the resurrection of the witch
I saw when I was a child

a wizened old crone
staring at me

changed into a mad thing
bird transformed.

I am not pure

I am not pure
I am damaged
psychic assaults
from the vaults of history
made me a skeptic.

I did not ask to be born
this non entity resided
in the outer universe
of lost souls
I think I had enough
to grieve about.

I am not pure
I am damaged
my fairytale frozen deep in the woods
a dark mysterious wound
I had to fight to exist.

I was the last and was loved
I didn't ask to feel hurt
I can't recall
just a deep somatic slice
in my body
ripping me to pieces.

Love on a steep cliff

Stray skulls of bird
gnarly bog oak
that's what he left behind
this bare place

I sense a sentient being
crossed the threshold
came and went
almost unknowingly

his threads hang on my mind
like rafters
I am chaffed to the bone
cliffs unfurl

silver slivers of light
slice the horizon
seagulls shiver
I oscillate to and fro

between the winds
of love and fear
like a demented sea nymph
seeking truth

in ancient rocks
every crevice sings
russet brown ferns
reveal the ritual signs

of emotional heart surgery
while soft threads
of latent love
grow from the ruins.

A Love of Freedom

How fleeting like a hint of gossamer you are
shuttered childhood light
before boundaries marked fields
small parish rivers endless
estuaries full of hope
spirit lies on the horizon
where you sing of infinity
seagulls rise with you
even in the gloom of darkest cloud
you are possible
depth charged you are in my soul
this spark lit up my life
the shadow song by my side
always singing of freedom.

Trip Hop

Now the mood is trip hop
all funked out and beaming
a wild wind roars around the house
outside it's abstract jazz
in here it's all chilled out instrumental
no voice patterns follow
cacophonic saxophone on the perimeter
mythical ships lost at sea
storms and silence
rhythms guide me slowly
to the half light of poetry
rapping on the rafters
drops like acid sound
words like fresh wounds
melt around sounds
light fantastically
flies in the attic room
where the mood is trip hop for sure.

A Kuku poem on an 18th

for Jeaic

You are the highlight of your tribe
not faithless but full of mystery
fierce as the mighty bull in your five billion stars
you lose yourself in the challenge
totally in the groove you are the armada
of your own powerful destiny
your psy-trance is magic
the trip you take will not blow your mind
your feet buried in the dark earth
your body longing for sea water
deep primal rhythms run through you

bam! you are a man
the condition you are in is your condition now
ours is our family of origin
do not bow to emotional suppression
live kindly with respect and consideration
live to be true to life itself
love as love commands
so release yourself
for I cannot utter the incantation
never forgetting the warrior you are
the son of the warrior
always remembers where he came from.

Forked Tongue

She writes about it in the other language
this thing she loves
her tongue forked from birth
a salmon swimming two streams
simultaneous linguistic schizophrenia
the water is cold
she was growing weary
no one was listening in the other tongue

flippety switch
one for submerged dreams
pre-infantile primal utterings
from her birth cave
the tongue most native to her

the neon other was louder
she loved it too
save for the shame in speaking it
some constitutional guilt
cultural snobbery
anti realism
curse her for her betrayal

It's o.k. she'd say: I'm just interpreting
this thing I love
so you will understand
the water is running thin
no one can hear me from the cave
so I swim upstream with this thing I love
this thing I love is my language.

Ad hoc love poem

Mesmerized by flames
I dreamt of random French phrases
sounds like how you seduced me
in our own native tongue
how I curled around you like a comma.

I threw a lightening bolt
you ate us whole
poetry my potion
I gifted myself to you
we moved like free verse.

Smoke in our lungs
you played to perfection
while we wafted away
on a feast of illusion
like existential questions.

The warmth, the scent of turf
lights your absence
we became the remains of ourselves
particles of gold in the ashes
unfinished sentences hovering.

Etching of Mount Brandon

Not like its usual self
a slice of its magnificent form
shrouded in a cloud
like a Japanese etching
a floating being
whose impermanent existence
makes us ponder
about our perceptions
how we are perceived
constantly altering form
between cloud shaded light
existing whole
just out of sight.

Motherload

I loved like a mother
I wrote like a dervish
I worshipped my muse
I did it cause I wanted to.

Three Friends

Three women found
a fairy mound
where stream met sea
at twilight
the good people
told them to take
their shoes off
after all this was sacred ground.

Fading light
created an aura
the three women spoke
on the mound
of fear and loss
words among them
illuminated bits
of something broken.

But they were strong
weaving their lives
into something deeper
like the landscape
of the fairy mound
they stood on
pouring their hearts out
to the fairy folk for hearing.

Lioness

Like a lioness
lying in her lover's lair
everything took
a more liminal hue

essence became a shower of meteorites
falling half naked
their crown was a sky of jewels
being outside in the night
not lost in their respective darkness's

their skin smelled of earth
love craved their bodies
lit like an interconnected grid

she was weary of the hunt
though the fiercest warrior
she was quietly bewitched
by the kindness and chaos
of this incomplete myth

stars sparkled on their story
opening her mouth
deserts of endless golden sand appeared
she lay and gazed
like the lioness she was.

Dark Angel

It could have been a conversation
between two ghosts
trying to set their souls free

words like mirrors
of brightness and mystery
flowed like a loom
in a field on the side of a hill

sacred threads of bitterness and pain
fused with ease
for she was practiced with sorrow
he lit her up this dark angel

energy flowed in her
highly aware of his body
she buckled in fear
the moment was lost

he gave her hope
though she would probably never see him again
she gave thanks for the time

the half magic moment
of pure talk
its hard to be tactile
when you are a ghost.

Come on Up to the House

for all involved – in gratitude

Floating between boundaries
of fields on the side of the hill
the strange folk came
to build a straw and canvas home
for us to be merry in

packed to the rafters at nightfall
we listened with our hearts open
to songs of pain and sorrow
our bodies danced with tunes
so alive we nearly burst

to greet our neighbours
merry with delight
to meet angels of darkness
who wanted their souls set free

boundaries are strange places
the half light and the threshold
into fairy lore
lurks within us all

those nights between
An Chathair Bheag and An Chathair Mhór
spirits rose
with the madness of it all
for being alive
for being present

souls crossed
tunes spoke
songs cried

we came on up to the house
we were overjoyed.

Stray Death

after my father Caoimhín

Bones dry
memories left to
lie in peace
or haunt our dreams
like specters
in the night
unspoken words
fall with regret
on autumnal minds
bitterness strikes
in sharp wintry gusts
small loving moments
loosen themselves
under spring soil
but you will not return
our reflection deepens
internal enquiries rise
into stray detail
wondering if we missed
the portent of your demise
you will ever be
summer softness
at full tide.

Pearls from the Wisdom Tree

after my mother Edna

The pearls of wisdom
fall from the vanity tree
you were the last
to wear them round your neck
I'm afraid to touch them
draped so elegantly
on the branches
of a small feat of artistry

your voice is silence
your presence alive
woven beauty
pearls that adorned you
hang from me now
dressing my landscape

each threaded bead
a pearl singing love
from some ballroom of old
where you
and my father danced

you gave them to me
I never wore them
now my bead of pearls
carries remnants of your skin
while your deep soul
flies in the cosmos

I will treat these decorative things
with respect
I will dance with them
in some room
my fingers touching the strings

bringing your powerful energy
into current life force
floating like a sacred memory
from you into the ether.

ACKNOWLEDGEMENTS are due to the following,
where some of the poems in this collection first appeared:

"The Contradiction of Fertility": *Autonomy,* New Binary Press,
edited by Kathy Darcy, 2018

"The October Revolution": *The Scaldy Detail 2013*,
Scallta Media, edited by Maggie Breen

"Wellness": *Fé Gheasa:Spellbound*, Arlen House, 2016

"Forked Tongue": *Two Tongues*, Ponc Press 2017

*

My thanks to the Cill Rialaig Project.

DAIRENA NÍ CHINNÉIDE is a bilingual poet and author of nine previous collections of poetry in Irish, the most recent of which is *Fé Gheasa: Spellbound* (Arlen House, 2016). *Deleted* is her first collection in English. Her other Irish language collections include *An Trodaí & Dánta Eile / The Warrior & Other Poems* (Cló Iar Chonnacht, 2006), *Cloithear Aistear Anama* (Coiscéim, 2013), and *Labhraíonn Fungie / Fungie Speaks* (Ponc Press, 2015). Dairena has received numerous awards for her writing including Irish Language Literature Bursaries from the Arts Council of Ireland, Ealaín na Gaeltachta and a Patrick and Katherine Kavanagh Fellowship. She was Irish Language Writer-in-Residence for Dublin City University (DCU) for 2017-2018. She has performed her poetry at festivals and literary events throughout Ireland, Europe and the United States of America.

salmonpoetry
Cliffs of Moher, County Clare, Ireland

"Like the sea-run Steelhead salmon that thrashes upstream to its spawning ground, then instead of dying, returns to the sea – Salmon Poetry Press brings precious cargo to both Ireland and America in the poetry it publishes, then carries that select work to its readership against incalculable odds."

TESS GALLAGHER

The Salmon Bookshop & Literary Centre

Ennistymon, County Clare, Ireland

Listed in *The Irish Times'* 35 Best Independent Bookshops